M ent

Donated in celebration of
*Roni Tewksbury's 25th
Anniversary with West Georgia
Regional Library*
by Friends of the Neva Lomason
Memorial Library 2008

by

CATHERINE THIMMESH

Illustrated by

DOUGLAS B. JONES

★ ★ ★

HOUGHTON MIFFLIN COMPANY ★ BOSTON

WEST GA REG LIB SYS
Neva Lomason
Memorial Library

DISCARD

O9-ABI-792

For Paul—Always
—C.T.

For my wonderful partner, Fiona Richards, who contributed
time and talent to the illustration and design of this book.
—D.B.J.

Text copyright © 2004 by Catherine Thimmesh
Illustrations copyright © 2004 by Douglas B. Jones

Photomosaic illustration on p. 74–75 © 2004 by Rob Silvers

All rights reserved. For information about permission to reproduce selections
from this book, write to Permissions, Houghton Mifflin Company,
215 Park Avenue South, New York, New York 10003.

www.houghtonmifflinbooks.com

The text of this book is set in Mrs. Eaves.
The illustrations were hand-drawn with pencil on paper;
color was applied using Photoshop on the Mac.

Library of Congress Cataloging-in-Publication Control Number 2004001053

HC ISBN-13: 978-0-618-39666-5
PB ISBN-13: 978-0-618-97143-5

Printed in Singapore
TWP 10 9 8 7 6 5 4 3

"Who wants to be a science teacher?"

". . . a landscaper . . ."

"Or a brain surgeon?"

4

"When I grow up, I'm going to be the president of the United States."

Abigail Adams

1600 Pennsylvania Avenue: home to the president. And the president's spouse. With 132 rooms, 35 bathrooms, 28 fireplaces, and 8 staircases, the stately, enormous white house has plenty to offer the traditional homemaker. But many a first lady has ventured beyond the confines of the white stone walls of hostessdom and out into the political arena of presidential advisors, and have themselves left a lasting footprint—whether it be pointy-toed and spike-heeled or rubber-soled and loosely laced—on the very bedrock of America.

As early as 1776, Abigail Adams—the wife of John Adams, one of the Founding Fathers and the second president of the United States—refused to sit on the sidelines as a mere spectator while her husband actively played the political game. When the demands of John's work kept him away (which was often), Abigail sent him a steady stream of notes and letters—well over two thousand throughout the years—expressing her many views, opinions, and bits of advice. Even before John Adams was president, when America was still being formed and a governing constitution still being drafted, Abigail dipped her quill in ink and put it to paper in an effort to influence the new constitutional code of laws. In her most famous letter, of March 31, 1776, Abigail beseeched John:

"And by the way in the new Code of Laws which I suppose it will be necessary for you to make I desire you would Remember the Ladies, and be more generous and favourable to them than your ancestors. Do not put such unlimited power into the hands of the Husbands."

In his reply letter, John Adams pooh-poohed her plea—amused, though, that she was "so saucy." Abigail's appeal for fairness on behalf of the ladies of America was readily but kindly dismissed—nothing would be written into the Constitution that would grant women the right to vote or the right to own property. During her years in the White House, however, Abigail's persistent candidness prompted many political enemies to criticize her husband in the harshest terms possible: ridiculing him as being under the control of a certain "Mrs. President."

Edith Bolling Wilson

It was quite the ventriloquist act. The Edith and Woodrow Show: she talked; he, supposedly, supplied the words. She hadn't been elected, and her actions were illegal according to the U.S. Constitution, but for all intents and purposes, First Lady Edith Bolling Wilson was in fact the president. When President Wilson suffered a paralyzing stroke in 1919, Edith (secretly) stepped in and assumed the presidential duties.

"So began my stewardship," Edith commented. "I studied every paper, sent from the different Secretaries or Senators, and tried to digest and present in tabloid form the things that, despite my vigilance, had to go to the President."

She was the sole liaison between the ailing president and absolutely everyone—including Congress. All the presidential correspondence was filtered through Edith, sent on White House stationery and penned in her hand, beginning with the words: "The President says . . . "

For several months, she issued directives in the president's name: authorizing the sale of thousands of tons of wheat flour from the U.S. Grain Corporation to the Polish government; "agreeing" with the secretary of state about withdrawing U.S. representatives from Paris; giving the OK for representatives to sign a treaty with Bulgaria.

Although she steadfastly asserted that she "never made a single decision" pertaining to government matters, recent evidence (provided

by medical records) proves that claim was false. Not only did Edith Wilson pen the words "The President says . . . ," but she alone wrote the words—the significant decisions—
that followed.

Eleanor Roosevelt

~

She put the "first" in first lady. Hold her own press conferences?
She was the first. Deliver a weekly radio address? First again. Write a
daily newspaper column? You guessed it—numero uno. She also
delivered countless speeches, published hundreds of articles, and
wrote several books. She was Eleanor Roosevelt, and in the 1930s she
assumed the role of first lady as none before her had done. Eleanor was
a trumpeter of just causes, a tireless advocate for the underprivileged,
and undoubtedly the most engaged and politically influential woman
the United States had ever seen. Her immense popularity brought with
it unheard of power for a first lady—and she wasn't shy about using it.
Eleanor championed the advancement of women and made it a point
to consistently bring issues of women's equality front and center—for
the president and for the nation.

·◆·

*"There were times when a list of names suggested for appointment, to
serve as individuals or groups, would come out and there would be no
woman's name on the list," Eleanor explained. "Then I would go to
my husband to say that I was weary of reminding him to remind the
members of his Cabinet and his advisors that women were in existence,
that they were a factor in the life of the nation and increasingly
important politically."*

·◆·

Her reminding apparently paid off. It was her husband, after all,
who appointed the first woman to serve in a presidential cabinet.

And if Mrs. R. (as she was affectionately called) ever wearied of accumulating a string of "firsts," she didn't show it. After a twelve-year stint as first lady, she was appointed the U.S. delegate, or representative, to the newly formed United Nations—an official government post. Another first.

Lady Bird Johnson

Sometimes Mother Nature needs a helping hand. And Lady Bird Johnson just happened to have one available. During her term as first lady in the 1960s, she created the First Lady's Committee for a More Beautiful Capital, calling for the beautification of Washington, D.C. Eventually, her ideas were implemented and expanded to encompass the whole country, with a special emphasis on beautifying the nation's freeways. Large fields and small patches and scattered bunches of wildflowers sprang up alongside highways and dotted hillsides—sprucing up America the Beautiful.

"The Constitution of the United States does not mention the First Lady. She is elected by one man only. The statute books assign her no duties and yet, when she gets the job, a podium is there if she cares to use it. I did."

Lady Bird used that podium from the get-go, lending her voice to help advance the causes of women. She presided over regularly scheduled "Women Do-er Luncheons"—organized to bring women of achievement together to discuss a topic of concern, be it crime, education, or her pet interest, beautification. In fact, her commitment to beautifying the nation's capital arose from one such luncheon, at which experts openly discussed problems of the cities and brainstormed some possible solutions. When her husband, President Lyndon Johnson, returned to the White House residence at the end of each day, it's been said that the first lady's words were invariably . . .

·•·

"Well, what did you do for women today?"

·•·

Rosalynn Carter

In her first year as first lady, Rosalynn Carter racked up some impressive numbers: 18, 27, 259, 50, 15, 32, 22, and 83. Translated, that would be: foreign countries visited, American cities visited, private meetings attended, public meetings attended, major speeches delivered, interviews given, press conferences held, and official receptions hosted. Rosalynn Carter once described herself as *"more a political partner than a political wife."* As first lady in 1980, she was the first to sit in (and take notes) on presidential cabinet meetings. She also held weekly business lunch meetings with President Carter, was named the chairperson of the President's Commission on Mental Health, and advised the president on all matters. She even represented the president officially in Central and South America. Regarding that, a reporter once said to her:

"You have neither been elected by the American people nor confirmed by the Senate to discuss foreign policy with the heads of (other countries). Do you consider this trip an appropriate exercise of your position?"

Rosalynn replied: "I am the person closest to the President of the United States, and if I can explain his policies and let the people of Latin America know of his great interest and friendship, I intend to do so."

Hillary Rodham Clinton

During the 1992 presidential campaign, they joked that they were a two-for-one deal, a "blue-plate special": elect Bill and get Hillary thrown in. It was clear early on that if Bill Clinton became the president, his wife would not waste her many talents lingering on the outskirts of the action. As first lady, Hillary Rodham Clinton traveled the world advocating women's and children's rights, tolerance, and democracy. She was a high-profile, independent powerhouse—and she immersed herself in the frenetic activity of the presidency.

⚬

"I'm often asked if what I am doing in Washington creates a new role model for first ladies," Hillary said. "And I always say I don't want to create any new stereotype. . . . I want all women to be given the respect they deserve to have for the choices they may make."

⚬

In 2000, continuing to press the outer boundaries of what a first lady is—or can be—Hillary Clinton became an elected official in her own right as a United States senator from New York.

And in 2006, she was overwhelmingly re-elected to the Senate to serve a second term. As a senator, she has been a tireless advocate for middle-class families and a leader on homeland security issues. In 2007, Hillary declared: "I'm in." (The 2008 presidential race, that is.)

"I'm not just starting a campaign, though, I'm beginning a conversation—with you, with America. Because we all need to be part of the discussion if we're going to be part of the solution."

· — ·

Running for president. Yet another milestone for a first lady.

But Hillary Rodham Clinton was a different kind of first lady—a blue-plate-special-kind-of-lady—a good deal all around.

"And, of course, when you're eighteen you can at least *vote* for the president . . ."

"Yeah. Voting's good. You can vote. Now. Finally. After seven long decades of struggle."

Elizabeth Cady Stanton

In the beginning it was a handful of women with an idea to come together to talk about women's rights. And in the end, they were three hundred strong—bunched in a small church in Seneca Falls, New York, in July 1848. Elizabeth Cady Stanton—often credited with being the architect of the rights movement itself—organized that first women's convention in Seneca Falls. She drafted their official document, the Declaration of Sentiments and Resolutions, demanding publicly (for the first time) the right of women to vote and to be treated as equals with men.

"When woman understands the momentous interests that depend on the ballot," wrote Stanton, "she will make it her first duty to educate every American boy and girl into the idea that to vote is the most sacred act of citizenship."

The Declaration of Sentiments was modeled after the United States Declaration of Independence. The first sentence differed by only two words: *"and women."* Elizabeth Cady Stanton's gathering proved a smashing success. (Ultimately, though, it would take another seventy-two years for women to get the vote—with Stanton herself never able to vote.) But at the end of those two labor-filled days in July, a bright new arrival could be toasted to—for Seneca Falls had given birth to the women's rights movement and the United States would never again be the same.

·•·

"We hold these truths to be self-evident: that all men and women are created equal; that they are endowed by their Creator with certain inalienable rights; that among these are life, liberty, and the pursuit of happiness; that to secure these rights governments are instituted, deriving their just powers from the consent of the governed. . . . Resolved, That all laws which prevent woman from occupying such a station in society as her conscience shall dictate, or which place her in a position inferior to that of man, are contrary to the great precept of nature, and therefore of no force or authority."

—Declaration of Sentiments and Resolutions, Seneca Falls, New York, 1848

·•·

Charlotte Woodward

W hen she saw the notice reading WOMAN'S RIGHTS CONVENTION, Charlotte Woodward was just a young woman of nineteen or twenty working as a glove maker in New York in July 1848. She worked for pennies—and what little money she did earn, according to law, had to be turned over to her father (if she had been married, it would have legally gone to her husband). Eager with anticipation, she journeyed westward from her home by horse and buggy to Seneca Falls. And before long, Charlotte found herself smack-dab in the middle of the pivotal event that history would mark as the beginning of the women's rights movement.

"At first we travelled quite alone . . . but before we had gone many miles we came on other waggon-loads of women, bound in the same direction. As we reached different cross-roads we saw waggons coming from every part of the country, and long before we reached Seneca Falls we were a procession."

Charlotte was young and enthusiastic enough to make the journey that hot July day, and courageous enough to sign her name to the Declaration of Sentiments—publicly supporting what was a very unpopular idea. The many arguments against women's suffrage, or the right to vote, centered on a woman's "divine nature" as wife and mother and her "exalted" status in the family and society. Her "purity" and "frailty" of womanhood somehow made her unfit to vote.

Who could have predicted that it would take more than seventy years for those rights to be realized? Certainly not Charlotte Woodward Pierce (now married), who in 1920 (the first year that women were allowed to vote), herself at the age of ninety, must have wondered if the day would ever come. But it did. And she, alone of all the original one hundred people who signed their names to the Declaration of Sentiments at Seneca Falls, took one final journey for women's rights—to the ballot box to cast her first vote.

Susan B. Anthony

First, she was a three-cent postage stamp. Then, a fifty-cent stamp. By 1979, she became her own silver dollar. A tireless leader, Susan B. Anthony devoted her entire adult life to working for civil rights and for women's suffrage. In 1878, thirty years after Seneca Falls, she was the primary author of the Nineteenth Amendment to the Constitution (although she would not live to see it finally enacted in 1920). Introduced to Congress as the Susan B. Anthony Amendment, it effectively shifted the focus of suffrage from States' rights to a federal guarantee. She traveled extensively, giving endless speeches, organizing and attending rallies and conventions, exhaustively writing letters to Congress. And, for better or worse, she was the first woman arrested for voting (illegally) in a presidential election.

Susan B. Anthony and the other suffragists heard countless excuses for why women shouldn't vote: women weren't educated enough; they were too controlled by their emotions; they were too pure for the rough-and-rumble-tumble world of politics; they were too weak to make their way through the crowds to the voting box; and undoubtedly they would conceal extra ballots in their bulky sleeves, secretly slipping multiple votes into the ballot box.

·•·

"No matter what is done or is not done, how you are criticized or misunderstood, or what efforts are made to block your path," wrote Susan, "remember that the only fear you need have is the fear of not standing by the thing you believe to be right."

·•·

Today, the image of legendary leader Susan B. Anthony can be found on just about any souvenir-type thing imaginable: T-shirts, tote bags, mouse pads, posters, pencils, pins, postcards, coffee mugs, bookmarks, notecards, necklaces, tree ornaments, and dolls. Much of the memorabilia features her most famous quote—a statement that summed up not only her work, but her life: *"Failure is impossible."*

Sara Bard Field

The plan was simple enough. Drive from San Francisco to Washington, D.C. Along the way, stop to give speeches and gather signatures—and deliver a petition to President Wilson demanding women's suffrage. And so Sara Bard Field set out in September 1915 (along with two others) in cold weather, in a heater-less, drafty car. The roads were incomplete and difficult to pass, signs were few, and they had no map.

When the car broke down, they fixed it. When it got stuck—in the ruts, or the snow, or the mud—they pushed. When Sara finally arrived in Washington, D.C., after four treacherous months, the car itself had become a roving monument to the movement—plastered with suffragist stickers and slogans. She carried with her the petition: a cumbersome parchment scroll that now held the signatures of 500,000 supporters, gathered en route. When she unfurled and presented the document to President Wilson, it was said to have literally stretched for miles.

• • •

"I . . . had dramatically unrolled the great petition," Sara recalled, "and I had reminded the President that this came from the voting women, [in states where women had the state right to vote] or from the voting men in states where

women did not have the vote but who so approved of their getting it by way of the amendment, and it had impressed him. . . . We all agreed that it was an impressive meeting and an impressive gesture, but we didn't feel he'd loosened up enough."

•◆•

Still, when half a million people speak with one voice, it's difficult not to tune in; and President Wilson—for the first time ever—agreed to at least discuss the voting issue with members of Congress. Map or no map, a turning point in the movement had finally been reached.

Mrs. J. L. Burn

In a way, it's fitting that it all came down to a note from Mom. Mrs. J. L. Burn, in a letter to her son, Congressman Harry Burn, wrote, "Hurrah! And vote for suffrage and don't keep them in doubt. . . . Don't forget to be a good boy and help Mrs. Catt [one of the movement's leaders] put 'Rat' in Ratification."

The Nineteenth Amendment to the Constitution—granting women the federal right to vote—had, with much drama and uncertainty, finally passed the U.S. Senate and

a reporter. "No woman has gone to the White House . . . in a senior position in the Congress to sit at the table with the President, to discuss the issues facing our country and the President's agenda."

·—·

And if anything should happen to the president, the Speaker is second in line (after the vice president) for succession to the presidency. With every election, the seats at the president's table are continually rearranged; but women leaders—thanks in no small part to Speaker Pelosi—are increasingly winning the right to pull up a chair.

"Secretary of State Madeleine Albright once said that for a long time, in years past, 'the only way a woman could truly make her foreign policy views felt was by marrying a diplomat and then pouring tea on an offending ambassador's lap.'"

Frances Perkins

Perhaps if she knew they would one day name a building after her (The Frances Perkins Building at 200 Constitution Avenue) she wouldn't have been so reluctant to accept the position in the first place—wouldn't have tried to resign at the completion of each four-year term. But eventually Frances Perkins did agree to serve as secretary of labor (four times) on the condition that President Franklin Delano Roosevelt would back sweeping changes in labor legislation. He consented, and thus Frances Perkins became the first woman appointed to a presidential cabinet.

> "The door might not be opened to a woman again for a long, long time," Frances Perkins said, "and I had a kind of duty to other women to walk in and sit down on the chair that was offered, and so establish the right of others long hence and far distant in geography to sit in the high seats."

She was called "Madam Secretary" by her colleagues. And per her agreement, Madam Secretary swept: she created measures that over-hauled employment services (providing free help for the jobless), created a minimum wage and a maximum hours limit, implemented unemployment insurance and social security, and ended child labor. Every American who has a job today benefits from the labor of Madam Secretary Perkins. Frances Perkins also played an integral role in developing the core ideas comprising FDR's now famous New Deal—including the immensely successful Public Works Administration, which is generally credited with the country's economic recovery from the Great Depression.

Frances Perkins was appointed to the cabinet in 1933. Twenty years would pass before another woman would be given a Secretary title. Today, though, gradually, more women are walking through the presidential-appointment-door—the one so dutifully and kindly propped open by Madam Secretary Perkins—women who are eager and able to claim the high seats within.

Madeleine Albright

⁓

Madeleine K. Albright was like Technicolor television. When in 1996 she was appointed the first woman secretary of state, she blew away the ho-hum days of black-and-white, pinstriped, buttoned-down foreign diplomacy. She arrived clad in a plethora of vivid colors: cobalt, crimson, cucumber green. She was hailed as the "most powerful woman in the world": she who spoke five languages; she who was a single mother, an immigrant, a refugee; she of the pithy one-liners, of the snappy rejoinders; she of the silken scarves and jazzy jewelry.

·◆·

"Because of my background, I grew up always interested in foreign policy," Madeleine remarked. "And when I was in whatever school I moved to, I would always start an international relations club and make myself president. But despite all that, I never, ever dreamt that I could be Secretary of State. And it's not that I was particularly modest, but that I had never seen a Secretary of State in a skirt."

·◆·

In her performance as secretary of state, she served as the principal advisor to the president on foreign policy and was primarily responsible for representing U.S. interests abroad. For example, she helped negotiate the Oslo peace accords between the Israelis and Palestinians. And, just as important, Madeleine Albright established that foreign leaders would, in fact, deal respectfully with a U.S. representative regardless of gender.

·◆·

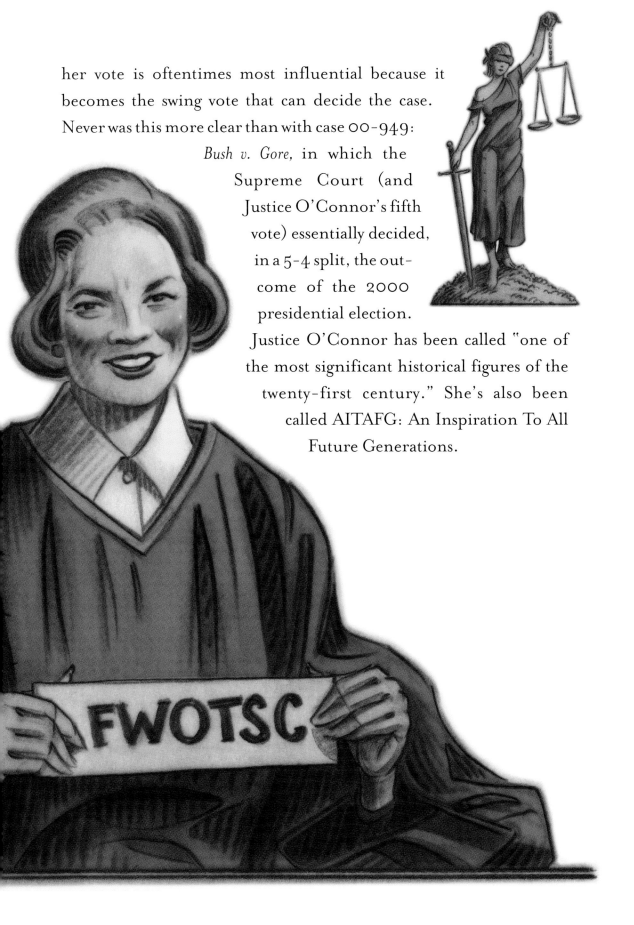

her vote is oftentimes most influential because it becomes the swing vote that can decide the case. Never was this more clear than with case 00-949: *Bush v. Gore,* in which the Supreme Court (and Justice O'Connor's fifth vote) essentially decided, in a 5-4 split, the out-come of the 2000 presidential election.

Justice O'Connor has been called "one of the most significant historical figures of the twenty-first century." She's also been called AITAFG: An Inspiration To All Future Generations.

FWOTSC

Condoleezza Rice

She is Teflon tough. Supergirl strong. But even the best of the best have weaknesses—and hers happens to be shoes: flats, pumps, spikes.

Make no mistake, though, she is powerful—a true force who just happens to sport Ferragamos. She has been described as the first and last: the first person the president meets with in the morning and one of the last people he consults with at day's end. Dr. Condoleezza Rice was first appointed by President George W. Bush to the key foreign policy post of national security advisor—the first woman to hold this high-level position.

Then, in 2005, she rose to the number one spot in foreign affairs—that of secretary of state—where it became her job to oversee and implement the President's foreign policy agenda. Condoleezza said her objective as secretary was to practice transformational diplomacy. At her confirmation hearing, she stated:

"We must use American diplomacy to help create a balance of power in the world that favors freedom."

As a child, Condoleezza dedicated herself to her academic studies (along the way becoming an accomplished pianist and a die-hard football fan as well), and she gained plenty of confidence early on to know that she could, and would, succeed.

"My parents," she once told a reporter, "had me absolutely convinced that, well, you may not be able to have a hamburger at Woolworth's [she grew up in the racially segregated South] but you can be President of the United States."

At the age of eleven, when visiting Washington, D.C., and the White House with her father, Condoleezza remarked, "One day I'll be in that house." And sure enough, thirty-some years later, she used her Ferragamo-clad foot to kick down the door of male-only-foreign-policy-leaders and stroll confidently and skillfully into "that house." The white one.

"We know you really want to be president . . .
but how about *vice* president?
That might be possible . . ."

Geraldine Ferraro

It was pure pandemonium. When Geraldine Ferraro remarked in her nomination acceptance speech at the Democratic National Convention in 1984, "If we can do this, we can do *anything*," the capacity crowd thundered its approval.

⋅•⋅

"By choosing a woman to run for our nation's second highest office," she said, "you sent a powerful signal to all Americans. There are no doors we cannot unlock. We will place no limits on achievement."

⋅•⋅

Almost immediately, Ferraro was buried under a deluge of letters—two or three *thousand* a day. Girls wrote saying that they wanted to vote for her—but couldn't because they were only ten years old. Women wrote saying that they wanted to vote for her—even though they had never voted before in their lives (and, by the way, could she please

give them instructions on where and how to register).
Many women wrote in secret, risking the ire of their
husbands and sending in campaign contri-
butions ("Please don't acknowledge this
gift," their notes would read. "My husband
doesn't know about it."). Vice President
Geraldine Ferraro. It had such a nice ring
to it. But being a novelty wasn't enough.

⋅–⋅

*"What I wanted to do was show the American people that I was qualified
to be Vice President."*

⋅–⋅

And she was qualified. She had served in Congress, gaining valuable
legislative experience; was well versed in the issues of the campaign;
performed admirably in the vice presidential debate; and communi-
cated comfortably with the voters. But in the end, presidential and vice
presidential candidates Mondale and Ferraro would lose the election.
In ceding the election, Geraldine Ferraro remarked:

⋅–⋅

*"Tonight the campaign ends. The race is over. My candidacy has
said the days of discrimination are numbered. American
women will never be second-class citizens again."*

⋅–⋅

That was more than twenty years ago.

Sirimavo Bandaranaike

In 1959, Sirimavo Bandaranaike was like a lot of women. Living in Ceylon (present day Sri Lanka), she was married, had three lovely children, and delighted in gardening. One year later, Sirimavo Bandaranaike—Mrs. Banda, as she became known—was singularly unlike any woman. She was now the prime minister of Sri Lanka—the first (and only) woman prime minister in the world.

Sirimavo Bandaranaike feels it's critical for women to assume leadership roles—for women's voices to be heard and for women's solutions to be implemented.

"Women's problems are not considered now . . . ," she said. "Women have to work very hard. . . . They have . . . problems that are different from what the men have."

In Ceylon, when her husband (the prime minister) was assassinated in 1959, Mrs. Banda campaigned for his political party—the Sri Lanka Freedom Party (or SLFP)—and in May 1960 became that party's leader. In the July elections, the SLFP won the majority of seats in the House of Representatives, and she, as head of the party, assumed the role and title of prime minister. She ruled for five years before she and her party lost power. She would return several years later, however, and serve once again as prime minister.

And, since then, while the closest the United States has come to electing a woman to the highest office was to have Geraldine Ferraro a vice presidential candidate two decades ago, at least twenty-eight other nations throughout the world have elected female heads of state (including three women from Muslim nations, which are traditionally male-dominated societies). Now, no longer is Mrs. Banda alone amongst women. In fact, she is in excellent company— including her very own daughter Chandrika, who in 1994 was herself elected to serve in Sri Lanka— as president.

Vigdis Finnbogadottir

In Iceland there existed for many years a generation of children who thought the president of a country was always a woman. That's all they'd ever seen, that's all they'd ever experienced.

Vigdis Finnbogadottir, or "President Vigdis," was elected the Icelandic president in 1980. Every four years, for twenty years, she was reelected to office. In Iceland, the president doesn't deal directly with legislation but does have the power to help form the government and is required to sign (or veto) all bills passed by the parliament in order for them to become law. The president acts as a negotiator in disputes and, most important, serves as a sort of "cultural ambassador" for the nation. President Vigdis has had a remarkable opportunity to influence and shape the position and perception of women in Iceland. And she's made quite an impression. One Icelandic girl wrote an essay on President Vigdis called "My True Hero," describing how growing up with a female president gave her enormous self-confidence and the belief that she could someday become someone important too.

"I'm convinced," remarked President Vigdis, "that the fact of a
woman winning the presidential election here will help women in my
country, as well as women in other countries. I can already see that
from the many letters I've received from women all
over the world. They've taken note of my election
and they think it's exciting and encouraging. . .
. It's time women stood together."

Margaret Thatcher

"Ladies and Gentlemen, I stand before you tonight in my green chiffon evening gown, my face softly made up, my hair softly waved . . . The Iron Lady of the Western World? Me? A cold warrior? Well, yes—if that is how they wish to interpret my defence of the values and freedom fundamental to our way of life."

She was tough—and rightfully proud of it. As Great Britain's first female prime minister (thrice elected), Margaret Thatcher took the Brits—indeed, the world—by storm, immediately dispelling the myth that women leaders were somehow weak. As someone who had always held strong views, it was only natural for Margaret Thatcher to seek out a career in politics. She was first elected to the British House of Commons in the Tory (Conservative) Party in 1959. Fifteen years later, she became the head of the party. When the Tories won the election in 1979, Margaret Thatcher, as leader, ascended to the top post of prime minister—where she governed for twelve years. Her economic policy, referred to as "Thatcherism," transformed Great Britain from a country on the brink of economic disaster to the current monetary powerhouse of the European community.

Prime Minister Thatcher's infamous "iron-willed" leadership style pieced together the very fabric of the modern British society. Only who knew it would be in green chiffon?

Benazir Bhutto

"I'm often told, don't be so soft. Be tougher. And I think that is perhaps the distinction between a male leader and a woman leader . . . ," explained Benazir Bhutto. "[But] they don't mean tough, they mean more ruthless. . . . Being nice should never be perceived as being weak. It's not a sign of weakness, it's a sign of courtesy, manners, grace. . . . I believe that we should be nice to each other, and I tolerate a lot of nonsense because I like to be nice to people."

When Benazir Bhutto became the prime minister of Pakistan in 1988, she was already only too familiar with the roller-coaster ride of Pakistani politics. The military had ousted her prime minister father in a coup, first jailing him and later killing him. Benazir was repeatedly placed under house arrest and jailed—oftentimes placed in solitary confinement in brutal conditions—for her protests regarding her father's unjust imprisonment. In 1986, after fleeing the country for two years, she returned and began to build up the Pakistan People's Party—a movement to bring democracy to her country. In 1988, she led her party to an election victory and she rose to the post of prime minister, becoming the first woman head of state in a Muslim nation.

Prime Minister Bhutto was famous for her unflinching confidence, and for embracing modernity and trying to meld it into Pakistani society. In 1990, she was dismissed as prime minister, but three years later she was able to regain control and again assume power as prime minister and rule for several more years before she was yet again removed from power and forced into exile in England. By 2003, though, she was publicly exploring ways to return to Pakistan, return to power, and regain the prime ministership. Unflinching confidence, to her core.

"Well, what are the rules for running for the presidency? What does the United States Constitution say?"

In Article II, Section 1 of the United States Constitution, the requirements— the prerequisites—for the presidency are as follows:

"The executive Power shall be vested in a President of the United States of America. He shall hold his Office during the Term of four Years, and, together with the Vice President, chosen for the same Term, be elected as follows:

. . .

No Person except a natural born citizen, or a Citizen of the United States, at the time of the Adoption of this Constitution, shall be eligible to the Office of the President; neither shall any Person be eligible to that Office who shall not have attained to the Age of thirty-five Years, and been fourteen Years a Resident within the United States."

"So, to run for president, a person has to be
1) an American citizen, born in the States,
and 2) be at least thirty-five years old.

Two things.
That's it. Right?"

"Umm . . .
right."   "She is absolutely
correct."   "Two things—
you're right."   "Yep. Two."

"Yep, that's it."   "Exactamungo!"

"After you, Madam President."

Timeline

1776

America declares its independence and the United States is born.

Abigail Adams asks Founding Father John Adams to "Remember the Ladies" in the new constitutional code of laws.

1848

First women's rights convention in Seneca Falls.

Elizabeth Cady Stanton writes the Declaration of Sentiments and Resolutions.

1860s

Women are granted the right to own property on a state-by-state basis.

1872

Victoria Woodhull becomes the first woman to make a bid for the presidency. She founded a reform party, the Equal Rights Party, and ran as their candidate. She began signing her autograph "Victoria C. Woodhull, Future Presidentess." She was highly controversial and never even got her name on the ballot.

1878

Susan B. Anthony introduces what later becomes the Nineteenth Amendment to the U.S. Constitution—giving women the federal right to vote.

Future Presidentess

1930s

Eleanor Roosevelt redefines the role of first lady with her active participation in White House matters. She reminded the president that *"women were in existence too."*

1931

Hattie Wyatt Caraway is the first woman elected to the Senate—though she is filling a vacancy left by her deceased husband.

1933

Frances Perkins is the first woman appointed to a presidential cabinet, as the secretary of labor.

1948

Margaret Chase Smith is the first woman elected to the Senate in her own right. She becomes the first woman to serve in both bodies of Congress.

1959

Sirimavo Bandaranaike of Sri Lanka is elected the first woman prime minister in the world.

1960s

As first lady, Lady Bird Johnson greets the president at the end of the day with, *"Well, what did you do for women today?"*

1988

Benazir Bhutto is elected the prime minister of Pakistan, a Muslim nation.

1988

Congresswoman Pat Schroeder set the wheels of a presidential bid in motion when she set up a formal exploratory committee. She remarked, *"When people ask me why I'm running as a woman, I always answer, 'What choice do I have?'"*

1992

First Lady Hillary Rodham Clinton comes to the White House in a "two-for-one deal." She is the first to have an office in the West Wing and the first to head a presidential task force.

1996

Madeleine K. Albright is appointed as the first secretary of state . . . in a skirt.

2000

When Elizabeth Dole announced her candidacy for the 2000 presidential election, she was seen by many as the first real female contender in the contest—the first woman who actually had a chance to win.

VOTE DOLE!

2000

Condoleezza Rice becomes the first woman national security advisor, and as such she is one of the first, and the last, people to see the president each day.

First Lady Hillary Rodham Clinton is elected to the U.S. Senate from New York and becomes the only first lady to be elected to high office.

1884

Belva Lockwood becomes the second woman to seek the presidency, also as the Equal Rights Party candidate.

1915

Sara Bard Field drives cross-country to deliver a petition to President Wilson with half a million signatures demanding a woman's right to vote.

LOCKWOOD FOR PRESIDENT!

1917

Jeannette Rankin is the first woman elected to either body of Congress. She serves in the House of Representatives.

1918

First Lady Edith Bolling Wilson secretly takes over the presidential duties when the president suffers a stroke.

1920

Tennessee representative Harry Burn follows his mother's advice and votes for ratification of the Nineteenth Amendment, finally giving women the right to vote.

Charlotte Woodward, one of the attendees at the first women's rights convention in Seneca Falls in 1848, votes in the election.

1922

Rebecca Latimer Felton becomes the first woman to serve in the U.S. Senate. She is appointed to fill a vacancy and serves for only two days.

1964

Republican senator Margaret Chase Smith runs for president in an effort to break the boundaries for women in the years to come. She remarked, *"An interviewer... asked how I felt a woman President would handle the other foreign leaders in the world. I responded... I thought a woman President would handle the other foreign leaders... probably... as well as Joan of Arc, Catherine the Great, and Queen Victoria."*

VOTE FOR MARGARET!

1972

Congresswoman Shirley Chisholm was serious about running for president from the beginning. But she got tired of telling that to reporters. Yes, she was a woman, and yes, she was black, and yes, she was serious. She said, *"I ran because someone had to do it first.... I ran because most people think the country is not ready for a black candidate, not ready for a woman candidate."*

1979

Margaret Thatcher, the Iron-Lady-in-the-green-chiffon-dress, becomes the prime minister of Great Britain.

1980

Vigdis Finnbogadottir is elected the president of Iceland, and a whole generation of children grow up thinking a president is always a woman.

First Lady Rosalynn Carter sits in on presidential cabinet meetings. She tells a reporter that she is the closest person to the president, and if she can help convey his policies, she intends to do so.

1981

Sandra Day O'Connor becomes the First Woman On The Supreme Court.

1984

Geraldine Ferraro runs for vice president of the United States on the Democratic ticket. She is the first woman to make it on a major party ticket. She and the presidential candidate, Walter Mondale, lose in the general election.

2002

Congresswoman Nancy Pelosi becomes the highest ranking woman in either body of Congress when she assumes her party's number one position—that of House minority leader.

Presidential Candidate

2003

Carol Moseley Braun, former senator, officially threw her hat into the ring for the Democratic presidential nomination. She entered a crowded contest, with ten candidates in all—herself and nine men. She stated, *"In these difficult times for America, I believe women have a contribution to make to move our country toward peace, prosperity and progress."*

2005

Condoleezza Rice is appointed secretary of state. She is the second woman to hold this high office.

2007

Nancy Pelosi is elected Speaker of the House of Representatives. She is the first woman ever to hold this position.

2007

Senator (and former first lady) Hillary Clinton declares her intention to run for president of the United States. She said, *"So let's talk. Let's chat. Let's start a dialogue about your ideas and mine."*

FOR PREZ!

Sources

Adams, Abigail. Letter from Abigail Adams to John Adams. March 31–April 5, 1776. Adams Family Papers, Massachusetts Historical Society archives. ("And by the way . . .")

Albright, Madeleine K. Remarks at White House Project Forum, New York, New York, Sept. 18, 2000. ("I believe that . . .")

——. Remarks to the Women and Co/Fortune Executive Summit, The Breakers Hotel, Palm Beach, Florida, Oct. 19, 2000. ("Because of my background . . .")

Brown, Drollene P. *Belva Lockwood Wins Her Case.* Nile, Ill.: Albert Whitman, 1987, p. 43. ("Why not nominate . . .")

Bush, Barbara. *A Memoir.* New York: Charles Scribner's Sons, 1994.

——. Commencement ceremony address at Wellesley College, Wellesley, Massachusetts, June 1, 1990. ("Who knows?")

Carter, Rosalynn. *First Lady from Plains.* Boston: Houghton Mifflin, 1984, pp. 201–2. ("You have neither . . .")

Chisholm, Shirley. *The Good Fight.* New York: Harper & Row, 1973, p. 190. ("I ran because . . .")

Clinton, Hillary Rodham. Keynote address at Scripps College, April 26, 1994. In *The Unique Voice of Hillary Rodham Clinton: A Portrait in Her Own Words,* ed. Claire G. Osborne. New York: Avon Books, 1997, p. 104. ("I'm often asked . . .")

——. Remarks at the 150th Anniversary of the First Woman's Rights Convention. Seneca Falls, New York, July 16, 1998.

Colman, Penny. *A Woman Unafraid: The Achievements of Frances Perkins.* New York: Atheneum, 1993.

Edsall, Thomas B. "Dole Opens Presidential Exploratory Effort." *Washington Post,* March 11, 1999, sec. A, p. 1. ("What would I . . .")

Ferraro, Geraldine. *Ferraro: My Story.* New York: Bantam Books, 1985. ("By choosing a woman . . ."; "What I wanted to do . . ."; "Tonight the campaign . . .")

Field, Sara Bard. Oral History. "Sara Bard Field: Poet and Suffragist." UC Berkeley, Regional Oral History Office. Interview conducted by Amelia R. Frey, 1979; available from the Online Archive of California. ("I . . . had dramatically . . .")

Frost, Elizabeth, and Kathryn Cullen-DuPont. *Women's Suffrage in America: An Eyewitness History.* New York: Facts on File, 1992. (Anthony, "No matter what . . ."; Mrs. J. L. Burn, "Hurrah!"; Harry Burn, "I want to state . . .")

Gelfand, David, et al. *8 Men and a Lady: Profiles of the Justices of the Supreme Court.* Bethesda, Md.: National Press, 1990.

Gurko, Miriam. *The Ladies of Seneca Falls: The Birth of the Woman's Rights Movement.* New York: Schocken Books, 1974, p. 99. (Woodward, "At first we travelled . . .")

Herda, D. J. *Sandra Day O'Connor: Independent Thinker.* Springfield, N.J.: Enslow, 1995.

Johnson, Lady Bird. The First Lady's Gallery, Lyndon Baines Johnson Library and Museum; National Archives and Records Administration, University of Texas. ("The Constitution . . .")

——. *A White House Diary.* New York: Holt, Rinehart and Winston, 1970.

Karlson, Katherine. "Women in Politics." *Binghamton University Alumni Journal 2,* no. 1 (Fall 2002). (Richards, "My grandmother . . .")

Levin, Phyllis Lee. *Abigail Adams: A Biography.* New York: St. Martin's Press, 1987.

——. *Edith and Woodrow: The Wilson White House.* New York: Scribner, 2001.

Lippman, Thomas. *Madeleine Albright and the New American Diplomacy.* Boulder, Colo.: Westview Press, 2000, p. 8. (Albright, "It used to be . . .")

Liswood, Laura. *Women World Leaders: Fifteen Great Politicians Tell Their Stories.* London: Pandora, 1995, pp. 25, 90–91, and 109. (Bandaranaike, "Women's problems . . ."; Finnbogadottir, "I'm convinced . . ."; Bhutto, "I'm often told . . .")

Margaret Chase Smith Library. A Biographical Sketch. Northwood University, Skowhegan, Maine. ("If I am to be remembered . . .")

Mayo, Edith P., ed. *The Smithsonian Book of the First Ladies: Their Lives, Time, and Issues.* New York: Henry Holt, 1996. (Johnson, "Well, what did you . . .")

Moseley Braun, Carol. Speech: "Peace, Prosperity, and Progress." Democratic National Committee Winter Meeting, Washington, D.C., Feb. 21, 2003. ("In these difficult times . . .")

PBS Online NewsHour with Jim Lehrer. Interview by Jim Lehrer of Nancy Pelosi. Feb. 7, 2002. Transcript p. 7. ("[In] over 200 years . . .")

Radcliffe, Donnie. *Hillary Rodham Clinton: A First Lady for Our Time.* New York: Warner Books, 1993.

Rankin, Jeannette. Oral History. "Jeannette Rankin." UC Berkeley, Regional Oral History Office. Interview conducted by Malca Chail and Hannah Josephson, 1974; available from the Online Archive of California. ("When I was elected . . .")

Roosevelt, Eleanor. *The Autobiography of Eleanor Roosevelt.* New York: De Capo Press, 1992, p. 132. ("There were times . . .")

Stanton, Elizabeth Cady. Address to The First Anniversary of the American Equal Rights Association, May 9, 1867. ("When woman understands . . .")

Stevens, Doris. *Jailed for Freedom: American Women Win the Vote.* Troutdale, Okla.: New Sage Press, 1995.

Thatcher, Margaret. "War of Words." Speech to Finchley Conservatives, Selborne Hall, Southgate, January 31, 1976. ("Ladies and Gentlemen . . .")

Thomas, Evan. "Condoleezza Rice." *Newsweek* (Dec. 16, 2002): 26–34.

Underhill, Lois Beachy. *The Woman Who Ran for President: The Many Lives of Victoria Woodhull.* Bridgehampton, N.Y.: Bridgeworks, 1995, p. 218.

Warford, Pamela Neal, ed. "Margaret Chase Smith: In Her Own Words." Margaret Chase Smith Library, Northwood University, Skowhegan, Maine, 2001, p. 104. ("An interviewer . . .")

Wagner, Dennis. "O'Connor Overwhelmed by Tribute." *Arizona Republic,* Sept. 5, 2002, online edition. ("Looking back . . .")

Weatherford, Doris. *A History of the American Suffragist Movement.* Santa Barbara, Calif.: ABC-CLIO, 1998.

Wilson, Edith Bolling. *My Memoir.* Indianapolis: Bobbs-Merrill Company, 1938, p. 289. ("So began my stewardship . . .")

Women's Voices: Quotations by Women. Quotes assembled by Jone Johnson Lewis. Online Women's History, womenhistory.about.com. (Perkins, "The door might not . . ."; Schroeder, "What choice . . .")

Wright, Ben. "Profile: Condoleezza Rice." BBC News, Sept. 25, 2001. ("My parents . . .")

Further sources consulted were the Adams Family Papers, Massachusetts Historical Society online; the Center for American Women and Politics (CAWP); CNN.com; the Council of Women World Leaders online; the Eleanor Roosevelt Papers, George Washington University; Ferraro's acceptance speech, 1984; the Frances Perkins Papers, Columbia University; the George H. W. Bush Library; Gifts of Speech, Santa Barbara College, online; Jeannette Rankin Foundation; Margaret Chase Smith interview with Joe B. Frantz; the Margaret Thatcher Foundation online; Runaway Technology; the online offices of Senator Clinton, Senator Dole, and Congresswoman Pelosi; the online office of the Supreme Court; the online office of the White House; the Stanton and Anthony Papers Project online, Rutgers; Steve Cotham, McClung Historical Collection; the United States House of Representatives online archive; the United States Senate online archive; WashingtonPost.com; and The White House Project.

The author offers a special thank you to Marie Wilson, Beverly Neufeld, Helen French, and The White House Project for their ongoing efforts to elect a woman to the office of the president of the United States and for their outstanding Web site (www.thewhitehouseproject.org), which provided a wealth of research material, as well as for their support and enthusiasm for this project. Thanks to Rob Silvers of Runaway Technology for his brilliant invention of the photomosaic, and for rendering my dream of a Madam President White House a reality—at least visually. The author also extends much appreciation and gratitude to editor extraordinaire Ann Rider for her expert guidance; and to Paul, Jaimie, and Simon for their support.

Index

Madam president
J 320.082097 THIMM   **31057010446105**

Thimmesh, Catherine.
WEST GA REGIONAL LIBRARY SYS